The French Verbs Reduced To One Conjugation: And Fewer Irregularities Than In Any Other System

Adolphe Loffet

THE FRENCH VERBS

REDUCED

TO ONE CONJUGATION,

AND

FEWER IRREGULARITIES THAN IN ANY OTHER SYSTEM.

Second Edition, Corrected and Improved.

By A. LOFFET,

GRADUATE OF THE FRENCH UNIVERSITY, AND LATE PROFESSOR OF MODERN
LANGUAGES IN THE ROYAL COLLEGE OF HENRY IV. IN PARIS.

" It may naturally be presumed, that an arrangement, which is perfectly new,
may possibly produce advantages which were entirely unnoticed before this
arrangement was actually drawn out; for experience furnishes us with a variety of
instances of unexpected improvements arising from new, and perhaps, fortuitous
combinations, which were never suspected by theorists, until a discovery had been
made."——WALKER, *Rhyming Dictionary.*

London:

THE AUTHOR, N° 12, MARGARET STREET, CAVENDISH SQUARE;
MITCHELL, ROYAL LIBRARY, N° 33, OLD BOND STREET;
WILLIAM JEFFS, N° 15, BURLINGTON ARCADE;
AND
ROLANDI, N° 20, BERNERS STREET.

MDCCCLII.

Works by the same Author.

———◦◦◦———

FRENCH AND ENGLISH PHRASEOLOGY;

BEING

A COLLECTION OF ALL THE IDIOMS AND REMARKABLE FORMS OF SPEECH
IN THE FRENCH LANGUAGE;

TAKEN FROM LESAGE'S HISTORY OF GIL BLAS, WITH THE
CORRESPONDING PHRASES IN ENGLISH.

One Vol. in 18mo. 1s.

———

L'ANGLAIS DANS L'ALLEMAND, ET VICE VERSA,

OU EXPOSÉ DES AFFINITÉS DE CES DEUX LANGUES.

One Vol. in 8vo. 2s.

LONDRES

DE L'IMPRIMERIE DE T. BRETTELL, RUPERT STREET, HAYMARKET.

AU TRÈS HONORABLE

LORD WARD,

FAIBLE TÉMOIGNAGE DE RESPECT

ET DE GRATITUDE,

PAR SON HUMBLE ET DÉVOUÉ SERVITEUR,

A. LOFFET.

THE FRENCH VERBS
REDUCED
TO ONE CONJUGATION.

———◆———

THE ENGLISH LANGUAGE, so rich in most respects, is nevertheless poor in the forms of its Verbs.

No English verb has, by itself and without the help of an auxiliary, more than two ways of denoting to what part of time the action it expresses belongs. Thus, *to pretend*, can only form the Present, *I pretend*, and the Past, *I pretended;* all other ideas of time are expressed by a circumlocution.

The French conjugation is more abundant, as it is possible, by simply changing the terminations, to represent the action of any verb in eight different points of view; so that in the conjugation of our verbs a single word often supplies the place of two in English.

———————

SPECIMEN OF FRENCH CONJUGATION.

INFINITIVE, . . .	*Prétendre,*	To pretend.
FUTURE, ...	*Je prétendrai,*	I will or shall pretend.
CONDITIONAL, . .	*Je prétendrais,*	I would or should pretend.
IMPERFECT, . . .	*Je prétendais,*	I was pretending or did pretend.
1ST SUBJUNCTIVE,	*Que je prétende,*	That I may pretend.
PRESENT, ...	*Je prétends,*	I pretend or am pretending.
IMPERATIVE, . . .	*Prétendons,*	Let us pretend.
PERFECT, ...	*Je prétendis,*	I pretended.
2ND SUBJUNCTIVE,	*Que je prétendisse,*	That I might pretend.

This fully demonstrates that in order to render such ideas, expressed in French by single words, the English conjugation requires the help of *to, will, would, shall, should, was, am, did, may, might, let*, words utterly different from the principal verb *to pretend*.

The foregoing French words are composed of two distinct parts, which may be thus separated :—

Prétendr $\begin{cases} ai. \\ ais. \end{cases}$

Prétend $\begin{cases} ais. \\ e. \\ s. \\ ons. \\ is. \\ isse. \end{cases}$ It is evident that *Prétendr, Prétend*, indicate the action ; and that *ai, ais, e, s*, etc. serve only to modify that action by the ideas of time, person, etc. etc.

Now, all the forms of any verb whatever can be divided in the same manner.

We must accordingly distinguish in every verb,—

The significant part, or *root*,	The modifying part, or *termination*,
which expresses the sense, the action of the verb, purely, simply, and disencumbered of all accessory idea; it is in each verb the initial part, such is *Prétendr, Prétend*, in the above instances.	which imparts to the action the ideas of time, person, etc. etc. It is the final part of the verb, such is, *ai, ais, e, s, ons, is, isse*, in Je prétendr-*ai*, Je prétendr-*ais*, etc. etc.

Thus, the art of conjugating French verbs consists in the knowledge of the *Roots* and *Terminations*.

The French language has at least 6000 verbs, each of which being conjugated throughout, will produce as many as fifty different forms or words. Of these fifty derivatives, the infinitive (the termination of which is either *r* or *re*) is the only one found in dictionaries.

Let us see whether it be possible to devise an easy plan for deducing from the infinitive, all the other forms of the verb.

OF THE FRENCH CONJUGATION.

The great difference which appears to exist between the conjugations of French verbs* is mainly attributable to a cause influential throughout the whole of that language, namely,—the blended pronunciation of every two words so intimately connected by sense, as to disallow their being considered separately.

---

* Some grammarians have admitted as many as twelve conjugations, and yet have been compelled to acknowledge a great number of irregular verbs.

Now, such a union of sounds being likely to produce discordance when two vowels are brought in contact, it has been found necessary to prevent their meeting, and the following means is employed :—

1st. Should the first word end with an *e mute,* and the second commence with a vowel, the *e mute* is suppressed. Thus, instead of—
Le aigle, quelque un, they say,—*L'aigle, quelqu'un,* the eagle, some one.

2nd. Should two other vowels meet, a consonant is interposed to prevent the unpleasant sound which would result from a clashing of the vowels. Thus, instead of—
Va il à Paris? A elle chanté? they say,—*Va-t-il à Paris? A-t-elle chanté?*
Equal attention was paid to euphony in combining the roots of the tenses with their terminations. By attending to this principle, the author has been enabled to construct a model of conjugation sufficient for upwards of 5900 verbs; and, as the few remaining, which the French language contains, differ only in some tenses, and no five of them are conjugated alike, he considers it unnecessary to construct other models, but shall offer some remarks to class their irregularities.

OF THE TENSES.

The French conjugation includes eight simple tenses; and two participles, the active and the passive.

To make the study of these ten divisions more easy, we may compare them to the members of a family, springing from one sire (the infinitive).

	SONS.			GRANDSONS.
	Future,	gives birth to		*Conditional.*
Infinitive	*Imperfect,*	,,	,,	*First Subjunctive, Active Participle.*
(Father)	*Present,*	,,	,,	*Imperative.*
	Perfect,	,,	,,	*Second Subjunctive, Passive Participle.*

NAMES OF THE TENSES.	ROOTS.	TERMINATIONS.					
		Je.	Tu.	Il.	Nous.	Vous.	Ils.
FUTURE, . . .	Porter Finir Suffire Rompre	*ai,*	*as,*	*a ;*	*ons,*	*ez,*	*ont.*
		Je porter-*ai,* tu porter-*as,* il porter-*a,* nous porter-*ons,* vous porter-*ez,* ils porter-*ont,*		je finir-*ai,* tu finir-*as,* il finir-*a,* nous finir-*ons,* vous finir-*ez,* ils finir-*ont,*		je suffir-*ai,* tu suffir-*as,* il suffir-*a,* nous suffir-*ons* vous suffir-*ez,* ils suffir-*ont,*	
CONDITIONAL, .	„ „ „	*ais,*	*ais,*	*ait ;*	*ions,*	*iez,*	*aient.*
		je porter-*ais,* tu porter-*ais,* il porter-*ait,* nous porter-*ions,* vous porter-*iez,* ils porter-*aient,*		je finir-*ais,* tu finir-*ais,* il finir-*ait,* nous finir-*ions,* vous finir-*iez,* ils finir-*aient,*		je suffir-*ais,* tu suffir-*ais,* il suffir-*ait,* nous suffir-*ion* vous suffir-*iez,* ils suffir-*aient,*	
		The root of all other tenses is formed by cutting					
IMPERFECT, . .	Porte Fini Suffi Romp	*ais,*	*ais,*	*ait ;*	*ions,*	*iez,*	*aient.*
		je port-*ais,* tu port-*ais,* il port-*ait,* nous port-*ions,* vous port-*iez,* ils port-*aient,*		je fini-ss-*ais,* tu fini-ss-*ais,* il fini-ss-*ait,* nous fini-ss-*ions,* vous fini-ss-*iez,* ils fini-ss-*aient,*		je suffi-s-*ais,* tu suffi-s-*ais,* il suffi-s-*ait,* nous suffi-s-*io* vous suffi-s-*ie* ils suffi-s-*aien*	
1ST SUBJUNCTIVE,	„ „ „	*e,*	*es,*	*e ;*	*ions,*	*iez,*	*ent.*
		je port-*e,* tu port-*es,* il port-*e,* nous port-*ions,* vous port-*iez,* ils port-*ent,*		je finiss-*e,* tu finiss-*es,* il finiss-*e,* nous finiss-*ions,* vous finiss-*iez,* ils finiss-*ent,*		je suffis-*e,* tu suffis-*es,* il suffis-*e,* nous suffis-*ion* vous suffis-*iez* ils suffis *ent.*	

EXPLANATIONS.

Future is formed by adding the terminations standing opposite to the Infinitive of the verb.

n the Infinitive ends with an *e* mute, that *e* must be suppressed, to prevent its meeting the vowels of the termination.

he whole of the French verbs there are but 23 Futures, which deviate from this rule.

mpr-*ai*,	I will or shall	
ompr-*as*,	thou wilt or shalt	
mpr-*a*,	he will or shall	
s rompr-*ons*,	we will or shall	carry, finish, suffice, break.
s rompr-*ez*,	you will or shall	
ompr-*ont*,	they will or shall	

Conditional is derived from the Future by substituting the terminations standing opposite for those peculiar to that tense.

he whole of the French verbs there is not one exception to this rule.

ompr-*ais*,	I would or should	
ompr-*ais*,	thou wouldst or shouldst	
mpr-*ait*,	he would or should	
s rompr-*ions*,	we would or should	carry, finish, suffice, break.
s rompr-*iez*,	you would or should	
ompr-*aient*,	they would or should	

or RE of the Infin.; thus in *Porter*, *Rompre*, the roots are *Porte*, *Romp*.

Imperfect is formed by adding to the root the terminations standing opposite.

e root ends with an *e* mute, that *e* must, of course, be suppressed.

e root ends in any other vowel, *ss* or *s* is interposed between the root and terminations, to prevent the clashing of the two vowels, thus: Je fini-*ss-ais*, instead of je fini-*ais*; and je suffi-s-*ais*, instead of je suffi-*ais*, &c.

.—*ss* is inserted when the Infinitive ends in *r*, as *finir*; and *s* when it does in *re*, as *suffire*.

mp-*ais*,	I was	
omp-*ais*,	thou wast	
mp-*ait*,	he was	
s romp-*ions*,	we were	carrying, finishing, sufficing, breaking.
s romp-*iez*,	you were	
omp-*aient*,	they were	

First Subjunctive is derived from the Imperfect by substituting the terminations standing opposite for those peculiar to that tense.

e whole of the French verbs there are but 18 Subjunctives which form exceptions to this rule.

omp-*e*,	I may	
omp-*es*,	thou mayest	
mp-*e*,	he may	
s romp-*ions*,	we may	carry, finish, suffice, break.
s romp-*iez*,	you may	
omp-*ent*,	they may	

NAMES OF THE TENSES.	ROOTS.	TERMINATIONS.					
		Je.	Tu.	Il.	Nous.	Vous.	Il
PRESENT, . . .	Porte Fini Suffi Romp	(s),	s,	(t);	ons,	ez,	en
		je porte,		je fini-s,		je suffi-s,	
		tu porte-s,		tu fini-s,		tu suffi-s,	
		il porte,		il fini-t,		il suffi-t,	
		nous port-ons,		nous fini-ss-ons,		nous suffi-	
		vous port-ez,		vous fini-ss-ez,		vous suffi-	
		ils port-ent,		ils fini-ss-ent,		ils suffi-s-e	
IMPERATIVE, .	„ „ „	—	(s),	—	ons,	ez.	—
		porte,		fini-s,		suffi-s,	
		port-ons,		finiss-ons,		suffis-ons,	
		port-ez,		finiss-ez,		suffis-ez,	
		qu'il port-e,		qu'il finiss-e,		qu'il suffis-e,	
		qu'ils port-ent,		qu'ils finiss-ent,		qu'ils suffis-e	
PERFECT, . .	Porte Fini Suffi Romp-i-	ai,	as,	a ;	âmes,	âtes,	èr
			s,	s,	t ;	-^mes,	-^tes,	re
		je port-ai,		je fini-s,		je suffi-s,	
		tu port-as,		tu fini-s,		tu suffi-s,	
		il port-a,		il fini-t,		il suffi-t,	
		nous port-âmes,		nous fini-mes,		nous suffi-	
		vous port-âtes,		vous fini-tes,		vous suffi-	
		ils port-èrent,		ils fini-rent,		ils suffi-re	
2ND SUBJUNCTIVE	„ „ „	(a)sse,	(a)sses,	(à)t ;	(a)ssions,	(a)ssiez,	(a
		je port-asse,		je fini-sse,		je suffi-sse	
		tu port-asses,		tu fini-sses,		tu suffi-sse	
		il port-ât,		il fini-t,		il suffi-t,	
		nous port-assions,		nous fini-ssions,		nous suffi	
		vous port-assiez,		vous fini-ssiez,		vous suffi-	
		ils port-assent,		ils fini-ssent,		ils suffi-ss	

* As the interposition of *i* or any other *vowel* cannot take place when the root, FINI, ends in a vowel, there is, in such verbs, no possibility of distinguishing (ex by the context) the Present from the Perfect; for instance:

EXPLANATIONS.

Present, no terminations are added in the first and third persons singular,
hen the root ends in an *e* mute.
se of the root ending in *any other* vowel, the *ss* or *s* must be interposed in
e plural, to prevent the clashing of the vowels.

np-*s*,	I carry, finish, &c.
np-*s*,	thou carriest, finishest, &c.
ap-*t*,	he carries, finishes, &c.
romp-*ons*,	we carry, finish, &c.
romp-*ex*,	you carry, finish, &c.
mp-*ent*,	they carry, finish, &c.

mperative has only three words: the first person plural, and the second, both
singular and plural, which are the same as the corresponding ones of the Present,
mitting the pronouns, *nous, tu, vous.*
ermination is, however, left out in the second person singular whenever the
oot ends in *e* mute, thus: *Porte* instead of *porte-s.*
apply the third person, in the singular and plural, we make use of the cor-
esponding forms of the First Subjunctive.
whole of the French verbs there are but 4 Imperatives that deviate from this rule.

p-*s*,	carry, finish, &c.
p-*ons*,	let us carry, finish, &c.
p-*ex*,	carry, finish, &c.
mp-*e*,	let him carry, finish, &c.
omp-*ent*,	let them carry, finish, &c.

e Perfect there are two sets of terminations. The first is used for the roots
nding in *e* mute; the second for all other roots indiscriminately.
the root ends with a consonant, as *romp*, an *i* is inserted between this and
the termination; or else the Perfect could not, in the singular, be distinguished
from the Present (*vide supra*), thus: *Je romp-i-s* instead of *je romp-s.*

mp-i-*s*,	I carried, finished, &c.
mp-i-*s*,	thou carriedst, finishedst, &c.
mp-i-*t*,	he carried, finished, &c.
romp-i-*mes*,	we carried, finished, &c.
romp-i-*tes*,	you carried, finished, &c.
omp-i-*rent*,	they carried, finished, &c.

Second Subjunctive is derived from the Perfect by substituting the terminations standing opposite for those peculiar to that tense.
his tense the *a* of the terminations must be cut off, when the root ends in any
vowel but an *e* mute.
, as in the Conditional, there is not one exception.

mp-i-*sse*,	I might	
omp-i-*sses*,	thou mightest	
mp-i-*t*,	he might	carry, finish, suffice, break.
romp-i-*ssions*,	we might	
romp-i-*ssiez*,	you might	
mp-i-*ssent*,	they might	

i-*s*, tu fini-*s*, il fini-*t*, mean { I finish, thou finishest, he finishes. Or, I finished, thou finishedst, he finished.

FORMATION OF THE TWO PARTICIPLES.

The Active Participle is derived from the Imperfect by substituting the termination *ant* for those peculiar to that tense. Example:—

Imperfect, . . Je port-*ais*, je finiss-*ais*, je romp-*ais*, je suffis-*ais*.

Active Participle, port-*ant*, finiss-*ant*, romp-*ant*, suffis-*ant*.

In the whole of the French verbs there are but *three* which deviate from this rule.

The Passive Participle is simply the root of the Perfect. Example: *Finir, suffire.* Perfect, *Je fini-s, Je suffi-s*; Passive Participle, *fini, suffi*.

If the root end with an *e* mute, that *e* is made acute. Thus, in *Porter*, the root of the Perfect being *porte*, the Passive Participle is *porté*.

Should the said root end with a consonant, an *u* is added. Thus, in *Rompre*, the root of the Perfect being *romp*, the Passive Participle is *rompu*.

SLIGHT VARIATIONS INTRODUCED IN SOME VERBS

For the purpose of preventing ambiguity, or avoiding such concurrence of letters as is contrary to the rules of French spelling.

(A.) According to the regular model of conjugation, the three persons singular of the Present of *Battre* ought to be such as follow: *Je batt-s, tu batt-s, il batt-t.*

Thus the *third person* would terminate with a *trebled consonant*, a conclusion quite contrary to the rules of French spelling, which does not admit of even a *doubled* one, *at the end* of a word.

This difficulty could not be removed by omitting the termination *t*, as *il batt*, a word ending with a *doubled* consonant, would still remain; and if we suppress two of these three *t*'s, the third person, *il bat*, will not be distinguished from the first and second, *je batts, tu batts*, by the termination only as in other verbs.

To remove all these inconveniences, when the root ends with *tt*, one of them must be suppressed throughout the singular of the Present, and no termination be added in the third person. Example:—

Je bat-s, tu bat-s, il bat.

From a similar motive, should the root end with a *d*, which is but the flat articulation of *t*, the termination *t* must be omitted in the third person. Thus, from *entendre* is formed *il entend*, and not *il entendt*.

(B.) In French as well as English the consonants *g* and *c* have two sounds; one harsh before *a, o, u*, as in *haranguer, caresser*; the other soft before *e, i*, as in *arranger, placer*.

Hence in verbs analogous to *arranger, alléger*, it becomes necessary to retain the *e* mute before the terminations beginning with *a, o,* and they write, *il arrange-ait, nous allége-ons,* &c. &c. For if the *e* were suppressed as in other verbs, the *g,* being then succeeded by *a, o,* would have its harsh sound, and it would be impossible to distinguish in pronunciation :

 Il arrang-a of the verb *arranger, nous allég-ons* of *alléger,*
from *Il harangua* of the verb *haranguer, nous allégu-ons* of *alléguer.*

It was also formerly the custom to preserve the *e* mute in verbs analogous to *placer, tracer.* It is, however, now suppressed ; but the soft pronunciation is indicated by placing a cedilla under the *c* (*ç*), and they write *il plaç-a, nous traç-ons,* &c. ; otherwise the *c* standing before *a* or *o* would have the sound of *k,* and it would be impossible to distinguish in pronunciation :

 Il plac-a, nous trac-ons ; of the verbs *placer, tracer,*
from *Il plaqu-a, nous traqu-ons ;* of the verbs *plaquer, traquer.*

(C.) On the other hand, in *vaincre,* in order to preserve the hard sound of the *c* in the tenses in which this letter would be immediately followed by *i, e ; qu,* which is the constant sign of the hard sound, has been substituted. Thus, in the Perfect, *je vainqu-is* instead of *je vaincis,* &c. ; and in the Imperfect, *nous vainqu-ions* instead of *nous vaincions,* &c. &c. The third person singular of the Present Indicative rejects the *t* of the termination : *Il vainc,* and not *il vainct.*

(D.) In verbs terminating in *er* immediately preceded by another vowel, as *plier, trouer,* a clashing of the vowels is tolerated, because in many such verbs the interposition of *ss* would give rise to an equivocation, as the following examples will show :—

If *ss*	*Lier,* they would be *je li*(ss)*ais,*	words which	*je lissais,* from *lisser.*
were introduced	*Plier,* *je pli*(ss)*ais,*	would be	*je plissais,* *plisser.*
in the	*Trouer,* *je trou*(ss)*ais,*	confounded	*je troussais,* *trousser.*
Imperfects of	*Dévier,* *je dévi*(ss)*ais,*	with	*je dévissais,* *dévisser.*

Euphony has therefore been sacrificed to perspicuity, and they write, *je li-ais, je pli-ais, je trou-ais, je dévi-ais,* &c. &c. &c.

(E.) No word ending in an *e* mute can have another *e* mute in the penultimate syllable. Agreeably to this principle of French orthography, verbs like *peler,* to peel, *mener,* to lead, *semer,* to sow, change the penultimate *e* mute of the root into an *e* broad (*è*) before the terminations *e, es, ent,* which are mute, and also in the Future and the Conditional. Ex. :— *Je pèle,* I peel ; *tu mènes,* thou leadest ; *ils sèment,* they sow ; *je pèlerai,* I shall peel ; *tu mèneras,* thou wilt lead ; *il sèmerait,* he would sow, &c. &c.

(F.) The same change is observed when the penultimate is *é* (*e* with an acute accent) as in *sécher,* to dry, *espérer,* to hope, *régner,* to reign ; that *é* becomes *è* (*e* with a grave accent) in the same circumstances. Ex. :—*Je sèche,* I dry, *tu espères,* thou hopest, *il règne,* he reigns ; *je sècherai,* I shall dry, *il règnerait,* he would reign, &c. &c.

(G.) *Y* is changed into *i* whenever in the conjugation it meets with an *e* mute; and we write *je paie* instead of *je paye*, &c., *je paierai* instead of *je payerai*, &c., from *payer*, to pay.

(H.) *Haïr* is conjugated regularly, but loses the trema (¨) over the *i* in the three persons singular of the Present, for the sake of distinction between Present and Past. Ex.:—

Je hais, tu hais, il hait, I hate, &c.

Perfect. *Je haïs, tu haïs, il haït,* I hated, &c.

(I.) *Bénir*, to bless, independently of the regular past participle *béni*, blessed, has also *bénit*, in the sense of hallowed.

IRREGULAR VERBS.

There are about seventy irregular verbs; in that number *eight* are particularly so, and must be committed to memory without any attempt at classification. These are: *Aller, avoir, être, faire, pouvoir, savoir, valoir, vouloir.*

CONJUGATION OF

être, to be;	*faire*, to do, to make;	*aller*, to go.
FUTURE.		
Je ser-ai, I shall be, &c*.	*Je fer-ai,* I shall do, &c.	*J'ir-ai,* I shall go, &c.
IMPERFECT.		
J'ét-ais, I was, &c.	*Je fai-s-ais,* I did, &c.	*J'all-ais,* I was going, &c.
FIRST SUBJUNCTIVE.		
que	que	que
je soi-s, that I may be.	*je fass-e,* that I may do.	*j'aill-e,* that I may go.
tu soi-s.	*tu fass-es.*	*tu aill-es.*
il soi-t.	*il fass-e.*	*il aill-e.*
nous soyons.	*nous fass-ions.*	*nous all-ions.*
vous soyez.	*vous fass-iez.*	*vous all-iez.*
ils soi-ent.	*ils fass-ent.*	*ils aill-ent.*
PRESENT.		
je suis, I am.	*je fai-s,* I do.	*je vai-s,* I go.
tu es, thou art.	*tu fai-s,* thou dost.	*tu va-s,* thou goest.
il est, he is.	*il fai-t,* he does.	*il va,* he goes.
nous sommes, we are.	*nous fais-ons,* we do.	*nous all-ons,* we go.
vous êtes, you are.	*vous faites,* you do.	*vous all-ez,* you go.
ils sont, they are.	*ils font,* they do.	*ils vont,* they go.

---

* *General Nota.*—The " &c." placed after a word denotes that the rest of the tense is formed as in the regular model (page 8), by the mere change of the terminations.

IMPERATIVE.

sois, be.	*fais*, do.	*va*, go.
soyez, be (ye).	*faites*, do.	*allez*, go.
soyons, let us be.	*faisons*, let us do.	*allons*, let us go.

PERFECT.

je fu-s, I was, &c.	*je fi-s*, I did, I made, &c.	*j'all-ai*, I went, &c.

SECOND SUBJUNCTIVE.

que *je fu-sse*, that I might be, &c.	que *je fi-sse*, that I might do, &c.	que *j'all-asse*, that I might go, &c.

PARTICIPLES.

ét-ant, being; *été*, been. *fais-ant*, doing; *fait*, done. *all-ant*, going; *allé*, gone.

CONJUGATION OF

Avoir, to have;	*savoir*, to know;	*pouvoir*, to be able.

FUTURE.

J'aur-ai, I shall have, &c.	*Je saur-ai*, I shall know, &c.	*Je pourr-ai*, I shall be able, &c.

IMPERFECT.

J'av-ais, I had, &c.	*Je sav-ais*, I did know, &c.	*Je pouv-ais*, I was able, &c.

FIRST SUBJUNCTIVE.

que	que	que
j'ai-e, that I may have.	*je sach-e*, that I may know.	*je puiss-e*, that I may be able.
tu ai-es.	*tu sach-es*.	*tu puiss-es*.
il ait.	*il sach-e*.	*il puiss-e*.
nous ayons.	*nous sach-ions*.	*nous puiss-ions*.
vous ayez.	*vous sach-iez*.	*vous puiss-iez*.
ils ai-ent.	*ils sach-ent*.	*ils puiss-ent*.

IMPERATIVE.

aie, have.	*sache*, know.	
ayez, have (ye).	*sachez*, know (ye).	[wanting.]
ayons, let us have.	*sachons*, let us know.	

PRESENT.

j'ai, I have.	*je sai-s*, I know.	*je peux*, I can.
tu as.	*tu sai-s*.	*tu peux*.
il a.	*il sai-t*.	*il peu-t*.
nous av-ons.	*nous sav-ons*.	*nous pouv-ons*.
vous av-ez.	*vous sav-ez*.	*vous pouv-ez*.
ils ont.	*ils sav-ent*.	*ils peuv-ent*.

PERFECT.

j'eu-s, I had, &c.	*je su-s*, I knew, &c.	*je pu-s*, I could, &c.

PARTICIPLES.

ay-ant, having;	*sach-ant*, knowing;	*pouv-ant*, being able;
eu, had.	*su*, known.	*pu*, been able.

CONJUGATION OF

*Valoir**, to be worth;	*vouloir*, to be willing.

FUTURE.

Je vaudr-ai, I shall be worth, &c.	*Je voudr-ai*, I shall be willing, &c.

IMPERFECT.

Je val-ais, I was worth, &c.	*Je voul-ais*, I was willing, &c.

FIRST SUBJUNCTIVE.

que	que
je vaill-e, that I may be worth.	*je veuill-e*, that I may be willing.
tu vaill-es.	*tu veuill-es*.
il vaill-e.	*il veuill-e*.
nous val-ions.	*nous voul-ions*.
vous val-iez.	*vous voul-iez*.
ils vaill-ent.	*ils veuill-ent*.

PRESENT.

je vaux, I am worth.	*je veux*, I am willing.
tu vaux.	*tu veux*.
il vau-t.	*il veu-t*.
nous val-ons.	*nous voul-ons*.
vous val-ez.	*vous voul-ez*.
ils val-ent.	*ils veul-ent*.

IMPERATIVE.

[wanting.]	*veuillez*, be so good as.

PERFECT.

je valu-s, I was worth, &c.	*je voulu-s*, I was willing, &c.

PARTICIPLES.

val-ant, being worth;	*voul-ant*, being willing;
valu, been worth.	*voulu*, been willing.

---

* The compound verb *prévaloir*, to prevail, is conjugated like *valoir*, except in the Present of the Subjunctive, in which it makes, que *je préval-e*, &c.

The remaining sixty irregular verbs are only partially so, as in almost all some tenses are regularly formed. Nay, there are even four derivative tenses invariably regular, namely :—

The Conditional, the Active Participle, the Imperative, the Second
Subjunctive.

Now as the terminations are the same * for all verbs, regular and irregular, it follows that difficulty can be experienced only in determining the roots of the five following tenses :—

Future, Imperfect, First Subjunctive, Present, Perfect,
and *the Passive Participle.*

In perusing the model of regular conjugation, we soon perceive :

1st. That the two first plural words of the First Subjunctive are exactly similar to the corresponding words of the Imperfect.

2nd. That the same words of the Present only differ by an *i* less in the termination.

3rd That the last word of the Present is similar to the corresponding word of the First Subjunctive.

Examples.

IMPERFECT, . . . *nous finiss-ions,* *vous finiss-iez.*
FIRST SUBJUNCTIVE, que *nous finiss-ions,* que *vous finiss-iez,* qu'*ils finissent.*
PRESENT, . . . *nous finiss-ons,* *vous finiss-ez,* *ils finissent.*

This remark may be extended to the irregular verbs; these eight words also correspond with each other*.

Boire, to drink, is one of the following list of irregular verbs,

IMPERFECT, . . . *nous buv-ions,* *vous buv-iez.*
FIRST SUBJUNCTIVE, que *nous buv-ions,* que *vous buv-iez,* qu'*ils boivent.*
PRESENT, ... *nous buv-ons,* *vous buv-ez,* *ils boivent.*

---

* With the exception of the eight verbs above given, which possess some peculiarities in the Present Indicative and First Subjunctive.

DEFECTIVE VERBS.

The following verbs are called defective because they are deficient in some of their forms.

Braire, to bray, is used only in the Infinitive *braire*, in the third persons of the Present, *il brait, ils braient;* of the Future, *il braira, ils brairont;* of the Conditional, *il brairait, ils brairaient.*

Bruire, to rustle, is used only in the third person of the Present, in the third persons of the Imperfect, and the Infinitive: *Il bruit; il bruyait, ils bruyaient; bruire.*

Choir is only used in the Infinitive and the Passive Participle, *chu.* See *déchoir* and *échoir*, in the Table.

Clore has no Perfect nor Imperfect, and consequently no 1st and 2nd Subjunctives. The Passive Participle is *clos.* The other tenses are regular. In the same way, *éclore*, to be hatched.

Faillir is only used in the Perfect and the Participle; both are regular. (See *défaillir*, in the Table.)

Frire has only the Future, *je frirai*, &c.; the Conditional, *je frirais*, &c.; the singular of the Present, *je fris, tu fris, il frit;* the second person singular of the Imperative, *fris;* and the Passive Participle, *frit.* The other forms are supplied by using *faire* with the Infinitive. Ex.: *Nous faisons frire, je faisais frire, je fis frire,* &c.

Seoir, to become, to suit, has only *il siéra, ils siéront;* Conditional, *il siérait, ils siéraient;* Imperfect, *il seyait, ils seyaient;* Present, *il sied, ils siéent;* Participle Active, *seyant.*

Gésir, to lie, to repose, has only: Present, *il gît, nous gisons, ils gisent,* he lies, we lie, they lie; Imperfect, *je gisais, tu gisais,* &c. &c.; Active Participle, *gisant.*

Luire, is only used in the third persons. The Perfect is *il luisit, ils luisirent;* and the Past Participle, *lui.* The other tenses are regular.

A TABLE OF ALL THE IRREGULAR VERBS.

INFINITIVE.	FUTURE.	IMPERFECT.	FIRST SUBJUNCTIVE. que	PRESENT INDICATIVE.	PERFECT.	PASSIVE PARTICIPLE.
Absoudre (see résoudre).						
Aller (see page 14).						
Acquérir*,	J'acquerr-ai, &c.	J'acquér-ais, &c.	J'acquièr-e, tu acquièr-es, Il acquièr-e, ils acquièr-ent, Nous acquér-ions, vous acquér-iez.	J'acquier-s, tu acquier-s, Il acquier-t, ils acquièr-ent, Nous acquér-ons, vous acquér-ez.	J'acqui-s, &c.	Acquis.
Assaillir†,	(Regular.)	J'assaill-ais, &c.	(Regular.)	J'assaille, tu assaille-s, Il assaille, ils assaill-ent, Nous assaill-ons, vous assaill-ez.	(Regular.)	(Regular.)
B Asseoir (see seoir, p. 18, and surseoir in the table)	J'assiér-ai, &c.	J'assey-ais, &c.	(Regular.)	J'assied-s, tu assied-s, il assied, il assied, Nous assey-ons, vous assey-ez, Ils assei-ent.	J'assi-s, &c.	Assis.
Astreindre, restreindre (see craindre).						
Avoir (see p. 15).						
Boire,	(Regular.)	Je buv-ais, &c.	Je boiv-e, tu boiv-es, Il boiv-e, ils boiv-ent, Nous buv-ions, vous buv-ies,	Je boi-s, tu boi-s, Il boi-t, ils boiv-ent, Nous buv-ons, vous buv-ez.	Je bu-s, &c.	(Regular.)
Bouillir,	(Regular.)	Je bouill-ais, &c.	(Regular.)	Je bou-s, tu bou-s, il bou-t, Nous bouill-ons, vous bouill-ez, Ils bouill-ent.	(Regular.)	(Regular.)

* So are conjugated *Conquérir, Enquérir, Requérir*, formed of the same radical. The radical itself, *Quérir*, is only used in the Infinitive: *Aller quérir*, to go and fetch.

† So is conjugated *Tressaillir*, formed of the same radical. *Saillir*, to jut out (a term of architecture), makes *saillera* in the Future. *Saillir*, to gush, is regular.

A TABLE OF ALL THE IRREGULAR VERBS—*continued.*

Infinitive.	Future.	Imperfect.	First Subjunctive. que	Present Indicative.	Perfect.	Passive Participle.
Braire, bruire (see p. 18).						
Ceindre (see craindre).						
Choir (see p. 18).						
Concevoir*,	Je conçevr-ai, &c.	Je conçev-ais, &c.	Je conçoiv-e, tu conçoiv-es, Il conçoiv-e, ils conçoiv-ent, Nous conçev-ions, vous conçev-iez.	Je conçoi-s, tu conçoi-s, Il conçoi-t, ils conçoiv-ent, Nous conçev-ons, vous conçev-iez.	Je conçu-s, &c.	(Regular.)
Clore (see p. 18).						
Conclure†,	(Regular.)	Je conclu-ais, &c.	(Regular.)	Je conclu-s, tu conclu-s, Il conclu-t, ils conclu-ent, Nous conclu-ons, vous conclu-ez.	(Regular.)	(Regular.)
Conduire‡,	(Regular.)	(Regular.)	(Regular.)	(Regular.)	Je conduisi-s, &c.	Conduit.
Confire,	(Regular.)	(Regular.)	(Regular.)	(Regular.)	(Regular.)	Confit.
Connaître§,	(Regular.)	Je connais-ais, &c.	(Regular.)	Je connai-s, tu connai-s, il connai-t, Nous connaiss-ons, vous connaiss-ez, ils connaiss-ent.	Je connu-s, &c.	(Regular.)
Construire‖,	(Regular.)	(Regular.)	(Regular.)	(Regular.)	Je construisi-s, &c.	Construit.
Contraindre (see craindre).						
Coudre,	(Regular.)	Je cous-ais, &c.	(Regular.)	Je coud-s, tu coud-s, il coud, Nous cous-ons, vous cous-ez, Ils cous-ent.	Je cousi-s, &c.	Cousu.

				Il cour-t, ils cour-ent, Nous cour-ons, vous cour-ez.		
Craindre¶,	(Regular.)	Je craign-ais, &c.	(Regular.)	Je crain-s, tu crain-s, Il crain-t, ils craign-ent, Nous craign-ons, vous craign-ez.	Je craigni-s, &c.	Craint.
Croire,	(Regular.)	Je croy-ais, &c.	(Regular.)	Je croi-s, tu croi-s, Il croi-t, ils croi-ent, Nous croy-ons, vous croy-ez.	Je cru-s, &c.	(Regular.)
Croître**,	(Regular.)	Je croiss-ais, &c.	(Regular.)	Je croî-s, tu croî-s, Il croî-t, Nous croiss-ons, vous croiss-ez, Ils croiss-ent.	Je crû-s, &c.	(Regular.)
Cueillir,	Je cueiller-ai, &c.	Je cueill-ais, &c.	(Regular.)	Je cueille, tu cueille-s, Il cueille, ils cueill-ent, Nous cueill-ons, vous cueill-ez.	(Regular.)	(Regular.)
Cuire,	(Regular.)	(Regular.)	(Regular.)	(Regular.)	Je cuisi-s, &c.	Cuit.
Décevoir (see concevoir).						
Déchoir††,	Je décherr-ai, &c.	Je déchoy-ais, &c.	(Regular.)	Je déchoi-s, tu déchoi-s, Il déchoi-t, ils déchoi-ent, Nous déchoy-ons, vous déchoy-ez.	Je déchu-s, &c.	(Regular.)
Déduire (see conduire).						

* So are conjugated *Décevoir*, *Percevoir*, *Apercevoir*, and *Recevoir*, formed of the same radical.
† So is conjugated *Exclure*, formed of the same radical.
‡ So are conjugated *Déduire*, *Enduire*, *Induire*, *Introduire*, *Produire*, *Réduire*, *Séduire*, *Traduire*, formed of the same radical.
§ So are conjugated *Paraître* and *Paître*, which latter is not used in the Perfect; but *Repaître* has *je repus*, and consequently, the Second Subjunctive *je repusse*, &c., and the Past Participle *repu*.
|| So are conjugated *Instruire*, *Détruire*, formed of the same radical.
¶ So are conjugated all verbs in *indre*, as *Astreindre*, *Ceindre*, *Contraindre*, *Feindre*, *Joindre*, *Peindre*, *Teindre*, &c. &c.
** *Accroître* and *Décroître* take no circonflex accent in the Participle Past, *accru*, *décru*.
†† The Active Participle of *Déchoir* is *déchéant*. *Echoir*, to fall due (formed of the same radical), is conjugated like *Déchoir*, in the forms which its limited sense admits of. The Active Participle is *échéant*: it has no Imperfect.

A TABLE OF ALL THE IRREGULAR VERBS—*continued*.

INFINITIVE.	FUTURE.	IMPERFECT.	FIRST SUBJUNCTIVE. que	PRESENT INDICATIVE.	PERFECT.	PASSIVE PARTICIPLE.
Défaillir,	(Regular.)	Je défaill-*ais*, &c.	(Regular.)	Je défaille, tu défaille-*s*, Il défaille, ils défaill-*ent*, Nous défaill-*ons*, vous défaill-*ez*.	(Regular.)	(Regular.)
Détruire (see construire).						
Devoir,	Je devr-*ai*, &c.	Je dev-*ais*, &c.	Je doiv-*e*, tu doiv-*es*, Il doiv-*e*, ils doiv-*ent*, Nous dev-*ions*, vous dev-*iez*.	Je doi-*s*, tu doi-*s*, Il doi-*t*, ils doiv-*ent*, Nous dev-*ons*, vous dev-*ez*.	Je du-*s*.	(Regular.)
Dire*,	(Regular.)	(Regular.)	(Regular.)	Je di-*s*, tu di-*s*, il di-*t*, Nous dis-*ons*, vous dites, ils dis-*ent*,	(Regular.)	Dit.
Dissoudre (see résoudre).						
Dormir,	(Regular.)	Je dorm-*ais*, &c.	(Regular.)	Je dor-*s*, tu dor-*s*, il dor-*t*, Nous dorm-*ons*, vous dorm-*ez*, ils dorm-*ent*.	(Regular.)	(Regular.)
Duire (see conduire).						
Écrire,†	(Regular.)	J'écriv-*ais*, &c.	(Regular.)	J'écri-*s*, tu écri-*s*, il écri-*t*, Nous écriv-*ons*, vous écriv-*ez*, Ils écriv-*ent*.	J'écrivi-*s*, &c.	Écrit.
Enduire, induire (see conduire).						
Enfreindre (see craindre).						
Envoyer,	J'enverr-*ai*, &c.	(Regular.)	(Regular.)	(Regular.)	(Regular.)	(Regular.)
Échoir (see déchoir).						
Élire (see page 14).						

Infinitive	Future	Imperfect	Subjunctive	Present	Preterite	Participle
Faillir (see page 18).						
Faire (see page 14).	Il fendr-a,					
Falloir,	Il faudr-a,	Il fall-ait,	Il faill-e,	Il fau-t.	Il fallu-t.	(Regular.)
Feindre (see craindre).						
Frire (see p. 18).	(Regular.)				(Regular.)	(Regular.)
Fuir,		Je fuy-ais, &c.		Je fui-s, tu fui-s, Il fui-t, ils fui-ent, Nous fuy-ons, vous fuy-ez.		
Instruire (see construire).						
Introduire (see conduire).						
Joindre (see craindre).						
Lire,	(Regular.)	(Regular.)	(Regular.)	(Regular.)	Je lu-s, &c.	(Regular.)
Luire (see p. 18).						
Maudire,	(Regular.)	Je maudiss-ais, &c.	(Regular.)	Je maudi-s, tu maudi-s, il maudi-t, Nous maudiss-ons, vous maudiss-ez, ils maudiss-ent.	(Regular.)	Maudit
Mentir‡,	(Regular.)	Je ment-ais, &c.	(Regular.)	Je men-s, tu men-s, il men-t, Nous ment-ons, vous ment-ez, ils ment-ent.	(Regular.)	(Regular.)
Mettre§,	(Regular.)	(Regular.)	(Regular.)	Je met-s, tu met-s, il met, Nous mett-ons, vous mett-ez, ils mett-ent.	Je mis, &c.	Mis.

* Redire, to say again, has, in the Present, vous redites (like Dire, vous dites); but the other compounds are not liable to this irregularity; thus we say: vous médisez, you slander; vous prédisez, you foretell; from Médire, Prédire. Maudire does not follow the conjugation of Dire, though derived from it. See that verb in the Table.

† So are conjugated Décrire, Circonscrire, Inscrire, Proscrire, Souscrire, Transcrire, all formed of the same radical.

‡ Se Repentir and Sentir are conjugated in the same manner.

§ For the apparent irregularity of Mettre in the present tense, see Battre, page 12.

A TABLE OF ALL THE IRREGULAR VERBS—*continued.*

Infinitive.	Future.	Imperfect.	First Subjunctive. que	Present Indicative.	Perfect.	Passive Participle.
Moudre,	(Regular.)	Je moul-ais, &c.	(Regular.)	Je moud-s, tu moud-s, il moud, vous moul-es, Nous moul-ons, vous moul-es, ils moul-ent.	Je moulu-s, &c.	(Regular.)
Mourir,	Je mourr-ai, &c.	Je mour-ais, &c.	Je meur-e, tu meur-es, Il meur-e, ils meur-ent, Nous mour-ions, vous mour-iez.	Je meur-s, tu meur-s, Il meur-t, ils meur-ent, Nous mour-ons, vous mour-ez.	Je mouru-s, &c.	(être) Mort.
Mouvoir,	Je mouvr-ai, &c.	Je mouv-ais, &c.	Je meuv-e, tu meuv-es, Il meuv-e, qu'ils meuv-ent, Nous mouv-ions, vous mouv-iez.	Je meu-s, tu meu-s, Il meu-t, ils meuv-ent, Nous mouv-ons, vous mouv-ez,	Je mu-s, &c.	(Regular.)
Naître*,	(Regular.)	Je naiss-ais, &c.	(Regular.)	Je nai-s, tu nai-s, il naî-t, Nous naiss-ons, vous naiss-ez, Ils naiss-ent.	Je naqui-s, &c.	(être) Né.
Nuire,	(Regular.)		(Regular.)	(Regular.)	Je nuisi-s,	Nui.
Paître (see connaître).						
Paraître (see connaître).						
Partir, sortir,	(Regular.)	Je part-ais, Je sort-ais, &c.	(Regular.)	Je par-s, tu par-s, il par-t, Je sor-s, tu sor-s, il sor-t, Nous part-ons, vous part-es, Nous sort-ons, vous sort-ez, Ils part-ent, ils sort-ent.	(Regular.)	(Regular.)
Peindre, poindre (see craindre).						

Verb						
Prendre,	(Regular.)	Je pren-ais, &c.	Je prenn-e, &c.	Nous pren-ons, vous pren-ez, ils prenn-ent.		
Prévoir, pourvoir (see the note on voir).						
Produire (see conduire).						
Recevoir (see concevoir).						
Réduire (see conduire).	(Regular.)					
Résoudre†,	(Regular.)	Je résolv-ais.	(Regular.)	Je réson-s, tu réson-s, il réson-t, Nous résolv-ons, vous résolv-ez, ils résolv-ent.	Je résolu-s, &c.	Résolu, résous.
Rire,	(Regular.)	Je ri-ais.	(Regular.)	Je ri-s, tu ri-s, il ri-t, Nous ri-ons, vous ri-ez, il ri-ent.	(Regular.)	(Regular.)
Savoir (see page 15).						
Scrire (see écrire).						
Séduire (see conduire).	(Regular.)					
Servir‡,	(Regular.)	Je serv-ais, &c.	(Regular.)	Je ser-s, tu ser-s, il ser-t, Nous serv-ons, vous serv-ez, ils serv-ent.	(Regular.)	(Regular.)
Suivre,	(Regular.)	(Regular.)	(Regular.)	Je sui-s, tu sui-s, il sui-t, Nous suiv-ons, vous suiv-ez, ils suiv-ent.	(Regular.)	(Regular.)
Surseoir (from seoir, p. 18),	(Regular.)	Je surseoy-ais, &c.	(Regular.)	(Regular.)	Je sursi-s, &c.	Sursis.
Taire (see plaire).						

* *Renaître* has no Participle Past.

† *Résoudre* has two Participles Passive; the first,—*Résolu*, meaning *resolved, determined*; the second,—*Résous*, meaning *dissolved*. *Absoudre* and *Dissoudre* (formed of the same radical) have no Perfect and only one Participle. *Absous, Dissous,—Absolu, Dissolu*, are Adjectives, and mean *absolute, dissolute*.

‡ *Asservir*, to reduce to servitude, is regular.

A TABLE OF ALL THE IRREGULAR VERBS—*continued.*

Infinitive.	Future.	Imperfect.	First Subjunctive. que	Present Indicative.	Perfect.	Passive Participle.
Traire*,	(Regular.)	Je tray-ais, &c.	(Regular.)	Je trai-s, tu trai-s, il trai-t, Nous tray-ons, vous tray-ez, ils trai-ent.	(Not used.)	Trait.
Tenir, venir,	Je tiendr-ai, Je viendr-ai, &c.	Je ten-ais, Je ven-ais, &c.	Je vienn-e, tu vienn-es, il vienn-e, Je tienn-e, tu tienn-es, il tienn-e, Nous ven-ions, vous ven-iez, Nous ten-ions, vous ten-iez, Ils tienn-ent, ils vienn-ent.	Je tien-s, tu tien-s, il tien-t, Je vien-s, tu vien-s, il vien-t, Nous ven-ons, vous ven-ez, Nous ten-ons, vous ten-ez, Ils tienn-ent, ils vienn-ent.	Je tin-s, je vin-s, &c.	Tenu, venu.
Tressaillir (see assaillir).						
Valoir (see page 16).						
Vêtir,	(Regular.)	Je vêt-ais, &c.	(Regular.)	Je vêt-s, tu vêt-s, il vêt, Nous vêt-ons, vous vêt-ez, ils vêt-ent.	(Regular.)	Vêtu.
Vivre,	(Regular.)	(Regular.)	(Regular.)	Je vi-s, tu vi-s, il vi-t, Nous viv-ons, vous viv-es, ils viv-ent.	Je vécu-s, &c.	(Regular.)
Vaincre†,	(Regular.)	Je vainqu-ais, &c.	(Regular.)	Je vainc-s, tu vainc-s, il vainc, Nous vainqu-ons, vous vainqu-ez, ils vainqu-ent.	Je vainqui-s, &c.	Vaincu.
Voir‡,	Je verr-ai, &c.	Je voy-ais, &c.	(Regular.)	Je voi-s, tu voi-s, il voi-t, Nous voy-ons, vous voy-ez, ils voi-ent.	Je vi-s, &c.	Vu.
Vouloir (see page 16).						

DIFFERENCE BETWEEN THE PERFECT AND IMPERFECT TENSES.

ONE of the greatest difficulties (the greatest, perhaps) experienced by the English who are learning French, is the right application of our two Past tenses, the Perfect and Imperfect; for, as the English language has only one Past tense, it affords no scope for comparison, and leaves the mind unpractised and unprepared to make such nice distinction.

The numerous rules set down in grammars, instead of throwing light on the subject, have only served to render it more difficult and obscure.

Rules having failed, we shall proceed in a different way, and attempt to elucidate the question by merely ascertaining the precise meaning conveyed by each form; trusting that, when it has been properly understood, it will no longer be possible to mistake the one for the other.

The tenses *j'étais, je fus,* both express a Past, and are both translated by *I was;* but here the resemblance ends.

The Imperfect represents an action as *going on* at the time mentioned, without particularising *when it began* or *how long it will continue;* while the Perfect expresses a Past, with the accessory idea that the action had *its beginning* at the time spoken of. Thus :—

Dieu dit que la lumière soit, et la lumière *fut* (Perfect).

And God said, Let there be light, and there *was* light (*i.e.* began to be).

Et Dieu vit que la lumière *était* bonne.

And God saw the light, that it *was* good. (Imperfect. Light was in existence; there is no idea of a beginning.)

Georges IV. *fut* couronné en 1821. (Perfect; meaning that he was actually crowned, that the coronation took place in that year.)

Georges IV. *était* couronné en 1821 (with the Imperfect, would mean that he was among the crowned heads at the time, without determining anything as to when his coronation took place, which might have been years before.)

A consequence of the indefinite meaning of the Imperfect is the use of that tense to represent an action as habitual, as often repeated.

Le seigneur du village *s'endormait* quelquefois à l'endroit le plus pathétique de mon sermon.

The 'squire *would* sometimes *fall asleep* in the most pathetic part of my sermon.——*Vicar of Wakefield.*

One peculiarity of the French Perfect is, that it can be used only when speaking of a time entirely elapsed; for instance, we may say, *J'écrivis l'an passé, le mois passée, la semaine passée, j'écrivis hier,* (I wrote last year, last month, last week, I wrote yesterday); but not *J'écrivis cette année, cette semaine, ce matin,* &c. (I wrote this year, this week, this mòrning); because this year, this week, this morning, &c. are periods in which we are still.

We subjoin the following passage of Lafontaine, as the best illustration of the meaning of both tenses.

Episode de Psyché.

La vieillesse en propre personne lui APPARUT, chargée de filets et en habits de pêcheur. Ses cheveux lui *pendaient* sur les épaules et la barbe sur la ceinture. Son front *était* plein de rides dont la plus jeune *était* aussi ancienne que le déluge.

Psyché le PRIT pour Deucalion et se mettant à genoux : " Père des humains," lui DIT-elle, " protégez-moi contre des ennemis qui me cherchent." Le vieillard ne RÉPONDIT rien. Il PASSA du côté ou *était* Psyché et l'abordant de fort bonne grace et avec respect, comme un homme qui *savait* faire autre chose que de tromper des poissons : " Belle princesse," lui DIT-il, &c.

Psyché ACCEPTA l'asile. Le vieillard la FIT descendre dans la ravine, marchant devant elle. La difficulté FUT de traverser le torrent qui *coulait* au fond : il *était* large, creux, et rapide. " Où es-tu, Zéphire?" s'ÉCRIA Psyché. Mais plus de Zéphire. Un pont portatif, que le vieillard *tirait* * après lui aussitôt qu'il *était* passé, SUPPLÉA à ce défaut. *C'était* un tronc d'arbre à demi-pourri, avec deux bâtons de saule pour garde-fou. Ce tronc *se posait* * sur deux gros cailloux qui *bordaient* le torrent en cet endroit.

---

* The Imperfect here expresses *what was habitual, what was often repeated.*

LONDRES:
DE L'IMPRIMERIE DE T. BRETTELL, RUPERT STREET, HAYMARKET.

CPSIA information can be obtained
at www.ICGtesting.com
Printed in the USA
386426LV00021B/198